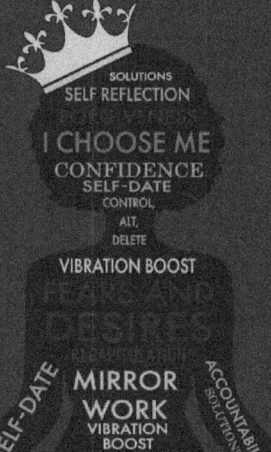

BUILDING A BETTER ME
THE TOOLS

Award Winning Author, Speaker and Coach
KELLEY R. PORTER

Other Books Written by Kelley Porter

- Perfectly Planned (Overcoming Incest, Rape and Sexual Abuse)
- Perfectly Planned Workbook (Guide to Releasing Pain Associated with Childhood Abuse)
- Overcoming Toxic Relationships (Creating Power from Past Pain)
- Detox or DIEt (Closing the Gap between Dis-Ease and Death)
- Mental MakeOver (Quote Book on life, inspiration, motivation, love and more)
- It's All About Life (Book of Poems) e-Book only

Building a Better Me:
THE TOOLS

KELLEY R PORTER, B.S., MSW Candidate

Copyrights © 2021

All rights reserved; printed in the United States of America. No part of this book may be used or reproduced in any manner whatsoever without written permission except in the case of brief quotation embodied in critical articles and reviews.

Designed by Kelley R. Porter
Cover Created by
Farrukh_bala
ISBN: 978-0-9851767-8-5

Acknowledgements

With love, honor, and gratitude, this book is dedicated to my customers, clients, and supporters that continually reach out to me for guidance on healing, confidence, and self-love. They are the reason I never give up as they remind me of just how great I am.

The **Best** Thing **I** Did Was **Be**lieve in **Self**.
Kelley "CoachKelley" Porter

Contents

Introduction

1. My Confidence ...   7
2. My Greatness ...   13
3. Not So Great ...   19
4. SMART Goals ...   25
5. Fears and Desires ...   31
6. Self-Date ...   40
7. Self-Comparison ...   46
8. Self-Reflection ...   57
9. Mirror Work ...   70
10. Control, Alt, Delete ... 82
11. Accountability ...   103
12. Focus on Solutions, Not Problems ...   114
13. Forgiveness ...   126
14. Set Boundaries ...   140
15. Recapitulation ...   147

Introduction:

What is Confidence? /ˈkänfədəns/

· The feeling or belief that one can rely on someone or something; to have firm trust.

· Trust, belief, faith, credence, conviction,

· The state of feeling sure about the truth of something.

· A feeling of self-assurance arising from one's appreciation of one's abilities or qualities.

Everything we need is already inside of us. However, most parents in this world did not teach that philosophy. Instead, parents and others taught us that everything external of us had more value and could help us reach any goal we chose. However, I ask this question and think about it before you respond. Were you taught to believe in yourself?

External factors help us reach our fullest potential, such as spiritual teachers, coaches, doctors, pastors, therapists, educators, etc. However, to achieve any level of greatness, you must have confidence that greatness lives within you. You must love and understand your value.

Humans teach us to believe in religion, the military and penal system, the healthcare and educational system, and man Gods. We are also led to believe in the Easter bunny, Santa Clause, the tooth fairy, Jesus, Allah, Buddha, the boogeyman, cinderella, doctors and lawyers, our pets, and everything else external of us.

We were even taught to believe in mainstream media: mere propaganda or programming; hence, the phrase, radio, and television '*programming*' station. Have you ever been told, "but the news said?"

So, I will ask you again, who taught you to believe in and value yourself and when? Did anyone in your childhood say you need to believe in yourself? Did anyone tell you how to believe in yourself? Did anyone say you are worthy or valuable? Or did you humans tell you to believe in Jesus? Now, I am not discrediting who you believe in, but should you not believe in yourself? Why are we fixating on external beings or things to help us reach whatever destination we desire? For instance, many women and men say, "I'm waiting on God to send my wife or husband." Humans say, when I get this job, I will be happy. Why are you no happy already? Do you not believe you can be satisfied without a job? Do not you think you were born with gifts? Some of us say I will never have what I desire, and I guess you never will because that is what you believe.

Who helped you understand that greatness lives in you and that all you must do is tap into it? Many of us say, "When I see it. I will believe it." How about you believe it, so whatever that thing is shows up. Believe it, and you will see it.

The best thing I ever did was believe in myself. I did not just write six books. Everything I experienced was *for* me so that I could write six books. Religion gears us away from believing in our higher self or the God within. There is another person within all of us that knows how to get things done. It is time for us to tap into that person and access the best parts of us.

Within this book, I documented numerous ways to build a better you. I have shared this information with clients and audiences, and now I am sharing them with you. I challenge you to act and start valuing yourself so that you can create your best self.

Every tool you read is one that I have used to build a better me; although there are more, I chose to share those listed within this book. In the meantime, get ready to build a better you through learn how not to crush your confidence but crush your goals.

Remember, confidence is the belief in you, having faith in yourself or something or someone else. If you do not believe in yourself, how will you get anything done? Everything starts with you, and if you have not accessed your greatness, you will find yourself "hating" on everyone that has. Believing in others is evenly necessary as believing in you.

One last thing; when was the last time you praised yourself, patted yourself on the back, took yourself on a date, congratulated yourself, or complimented yourself. Or are you stuck in that space where you still believe it is arrogant or vain to 'love on' yourself; to look in a mirror, or are you one of those people who become irritated by people who look at themselves in every mirror they pass by? If you are stuck in that space, it's time for your breakthrough. It is time for you to remove your self-limiting belief system and broaden your perspective. Shift your paradigm. You may be five feet tall, but there is a giant within. It is time for you to stop projecting your limited belief system and insecurities on others. You are just as great as anyone else, but you must believe you are. I am confident that 'Building a Better Me' will propel your person to new heights.

Chapter One: My Confidence

My mother and father always told me how pretty I was, and I could do whatever I wanted. My dad said that *I could do whatever a man could and not ever let someone tell me what I could or could not do.* My father was adamant about teaching me to believe in myself, be independent and go for what I wanted. He called me a "go-getter." At 11 years old, I didn't understand what he meant, but he smiled when he said it, so it must have been something good. Upon learning what he meant; I discovered my father was right; he knew his daughter. I must have mirrored some of his behaviors. Besides being 48 years older than me, we are both Leos and born ten days apart.

A go-getter is one with great initiative, a 'hustler,' motivated, or a powerhouse that knows what they desire, will never settle for less or stop until they achieve the goal. My dad was right, and still, to this day, I am that woman. However, what does that have to do with my confidence? I will get to that in a moment. My mother always told me I had a good heart and to always help people. So, throughout grammar school, I tutored classes like language arts and math. In college, I tutored organic chemistry and english. Today, I am a Life and Wellness Coach, legendary Author and Professional Speaker. I spent my entire professional career helping others create better health and become better people.

 I entered the healthcare arena because my father encouraged me to, and for many years, I thought I lived his dream, but it was all for me. I now understand the connection between my past career as a phlebotomist, laboratory scientist and my current purpose as a certified life and wellness coach. I thought working in healthcare for over 23 years was a waste of time. However, it was not as it helps to be a science major to teach natural healing, understand the body, and how what we ingest creates dis-ease or heals the body. That leads me to my mom sharing the importance of helping others.

Obtaining my master's degree in social work (therapist, policy advocate, and educator) aligns with my life's purpose; covering all aspects of the human being, mind, body, and soul, I am living out what my mom and dad saw in me. My parents were right, and everything they told me about me was accurate. It was all in divine order. Everything I experienced from incest, rape and sexual abuse, domestic violence relationships, two attempted suicides, and time in mental institutions were all FOR my highest good. All the education I obtained and am currently getting was and is for my highest good.

So, what does this have to do with confidence? My parents saw something in me that I was incapable of seeing at that time and with their love and guidance, all my experiences, education, and so forth led me to understand that all things are FOR me and not TO me. That said, I have no choice but to believe in myself. When you believe in yourself, you have no choice but to shine. I have been a beacon of light to humans all my life and am where I am supposed to be.

Not one thing that I experienced in this lifetime was to me but for me. I believe that, as I hope every tool shared experience in this book guides you to consider and value yourself and understand that nothing happens to you but for you. Life is for us.

In essence, I was born with an immense amount of confidence, and so were you. Humans help you to see it or crush it. When my parents separated, I felt destroyed and lost without them. I was angry, hurt, betrayed, and sad. Throughout high school, I did not believe in myself. I lost confidence in myself and did poorly in school. The abuse I experienced did not help either; however, my parents' words built me. And I still hear those words today. Even throughout junior college, my self-confidence was exceptionally low to a certain extinct. In school, I did horrible compared to how I started. However, as a dancer (stripper), I did very well, and numerous people paid me to travel, dance, and entertain. My belief in my dancing abilities was firm. As a patient care technician, I did a fantastic job, and many of the nurses and doctors at the University of Chicago hospital believed in my abilities. They all wanted me to go back to school for nursing as my dad did, but I did not feel I could graduate from college as I had not witnessed that in my family. Although my dad told me to go to college, no one told me what the experience would be like, so I did not believe I could do it. I say that to say this; confidence varies based on your areas of strengths. In some areas, you feel better and others not so much. And that is ok; however, the same confidence it took you to reach your highest goal is the same confidence you will apply to every area of your life.

Lastly, ten years ago, if someone had told me I would write books, start my own business, and speak at some prestigious organizations, I would have told them they were lying. Well, here I am. However, my confidence in running a business was not so high. I am still learning today and getting better each day. So, let me introduce you to what is great about me. Well, at least a few attributes as there are many.

Chapter Three: My Greatness

You might think this is an easy one; however, this upcoming task is difficult when people do not believe in themselves. The goal here is to identify the great things about you. Again, if you do not believe in or value yourself, you might not be able to recognize anything, or it may be challenging to do so. What is more, if you can write great things about yourself, chances are, you will begin to believe them. Before I share ten positive things about me, let me share why this process is essential and how. Not only will you document these great things about yourself, but you will read and acknowledge yourself for your attributes.

These attributes not only benefit you, but they help those people in your circle as well. Positive features mean positive energy, and positive energy means feeling good, and feeling good means getting stuff done. Can you see that? If not, let me share my ten positive attributes and break those down for you. I want to give you an idea of what sharing positive things about yourself can help you. Here we go.

- I love helping others.
- I am transparent.
- I am organized.
- I am energetic.
- I am passionate.
- I am trustworthy.
- I am honest.
- I am determined.
- I am loyal.
- I am vulnerable.

Now, imagine if I did not believe those things to be true about me. I would probably walk around with my head hanging low. I would become how others defined me. When you do not believe in yourself, you have no idea who you are. It is then easy for others to determine you by either crushing your confidence or building it.

Let us go back to my ten positive attributes or characteristics. First, I love helping others, and it makes me feel good. When we help other people, we raise our vibrations. Raising your vibrations means raising your energy or **e**nergy in **m**otion (**em**otions). Boosting your energy means feeling better, and once you feel better, you will find yourself doing more of what makes you feel better.

I am transparent. Most people are afraid to be, as many humans live in shame and fear what people think of them. I do not. Can you see the power in that? Being transparent makes me feel good about being me as it authenticates my confidence and empowers me to do more and be more. Transparency is empowering and freedom.

I am organized. Being an organized individual affords me to have a clutter-free life. If your home or workspace is cluttered, more than likely, your mind matches. Organizational skills require you to maintain order, plan, coordinate and manage. If you do not believe in yourself, there is no way you are planning or organizing anything.

For example, every season, I reorganize my closet to ensure that it is clutter-free. In my office, I have files, such as tax papers, birth records, degrees, and keepsakes, all in their prospective folders. Those may all seem like easy tasks; however, one who does not believe in themselves will not organize anything as they do not see value in organizational skills.

I am an energetic person. The therapeutic world calls it ADHD, and I beg to differ. I call it kinetic and potential energy stored as ATP or adenosine triphosphate. My attention span is normal, and my energy compliments it. I can hike mountains, jog a mile in 10 minutes, dance for hours, write books and facilitate workshops. I feel good as I document these positive attributes about myself. I am also a deeply passionate woman. If you have watched me on FB live or hired me, you understand my dynamic nature. A passionate individual is someone who has strong feelings or a strong *belief* in something. Hence, confidence and passion go hand in hand. It is a firm conviction, and no one can change your mind or persuade you to do or think otherwise. Why? Because you believe in your passion.

    Do you get the point? Do you understand how speaking positively about yourself makes you feel good? Imagine talking negatively about yourself. How do you think you would feel? Try that, and you will feel it later. Negative self-talk is a tad bit different. Negative self-talk looks like I am stupid, worthless, and will never have what I desire. How does that feel? Not good, correct. If speaking negatively about yourself makes you feel bad, imagine how talking positively about yourself makes you think and feel.

After you identify at least ten great things about you, write them down on a piece of paper, or even paint them on a canvas board and hang it on your wall. Then, read them daily until your brain automatically shares them with anyone that asks.

Chapter Three: Not So Great

Now, let us see how easy or hard it is to write 10 'Not So Great' things about you. Please, take your time with this. Do not affirm anything that you do not want to present itself in your life. What do I mean? I mean, do not speak it unless you want it. For example, do not use *I am* unless you are comfortable with the adjective that follows it. Remember, the words that follow 'I am' will follow you.

You might question the following tool, but this is a tad bit different than negative self-talk. What's more, I do not recommend we use the term negatively. Instead, we use not-so-great. I will start by sharing ten not-so-great things about me.

In my upcoming list, I stated I am straightforward. Well, that is the truth, and I am comfortable with that. However, if you look at impatience, I said I can be impatient, meaning at any given time, but not as an affirmation. In essence, do not document anything that makes you feel bad. Check out the examples below.

- I have trouble accepting love.
- I doubt myself often.
- I do not communicate well.
- I am sometimes afraid to be me.
- I need to believe more in myself.

Those are a few examples of some attributes or characteristics that you do not want to speak into the universe. Remember, this is not about negative self-talk or self-criticism, but about looking at your flaws or those things you might need to improve. If you cannot look at your weaknesses, it will be impossible to build confidence in lies and avoidance.

Would you please look at my list?

- I can be controlling.
- I can be impatient.
- I can be arrogant.

- I can be overextending.
- I can overspend sometimes.
- I talk too much.
- I am opinionated.
- I am straightforward.
- I interrupt humans while they are talking (sometimes)
- I can be judgmental

Some people may perceive some of those attributes as excellent to have, but on the flip side, those traits can trigger pain in others and cause conflict in relationships. If I feel bad about who I am or sabotage myself, I will lose belief in myself. Let's talk about a few of the 'not so cool' attributes.

Being dominant may push people away; however, if I am honest with myself, I become conscious and embrace, tweak or release that behavior. I have an alpha personality but being alpha does not always work in any relationship. We must be conscious of how our actions and characteristics affect others. Embracing these 'not so great' characteristics allows room for growth and increasing belief in self. It is okay to embrace and love your dark side or those parts of you that others deem as problematic.

We all know impatience leads to stress, and a stressed body causes the release of hormones such as adrenaline and cortisol. Adrenaline elevates your blood pressure, and cortisol increases sugars in the bloodstream and causes weight gain. How does excess fat or stress benefit anyone or raise your confidence? When I understand and embrace my impatience, it allows me to expand and practice being more patient. If I can improve my being and become better, doesn't that increase my confidence?

I am straightforward. Now, most people would like to say what is on their minds, and I do as I am brutally honest. However, it does not make it right, and it does not make it wrong. But what does happen is, being very blunt about my opinions can be disrespectful and hurtful to others or anger people. Now, I am not responsible for how humans react; instead, how I behave. Although being blunt is a natural part of who I am, hurting others is not. So being aware of my straightforwardness makes room for me to take a step back and analyze what I want to say and be more diplomatic versus just allowing words to roll off my tongue. At any rate, do you see my point? Those not-so-great things enable you to improve yourself, resulting in increased confidence. What is more, if you refuse to acknowledge those not-so-great things about you, that means you do not fully accept yourself.

So, go ahead and write down ten not-so-great things about you and once you have finished, walk away. Next, think about why it is important to you to embrace your flaws and fully accept yourself. After that, directly next to your flaw, write the trait you would like to have by starting with the words I am.

Chapter Four: SMART Goals

How many times have you set a goal and did not reach it? That is a confidence crusher, and more than likely, you probably never set that goal again. Unless you are as determined as I am, you tried again. When I started facilitating seminars about seven years ago, I was unfamiliar with the business game, and "failure" crushed my confidence. The first year was very successful, and so was the second year. The third was great, and the fourth year was terrific. However, that fifth year, I had to cancel the event as my registration was deficient. Low to the point where I would have taken a considerable loss, and my goodness, I felt terrible. However, I did not give up. The following year, my Silence No More Seminar was very successful. Painful experiences are great teachers if we seek the lesson instead of waddling in pity.

For this segment, I recommend you choose something SMART. According to the National Society of Leadership & Success, SMART stands for Specific, Measurable, Achievable, Rewarding, and Timely.

For *Specific*, create a goal that is specific and not broad. For example, if you desire to release weight, be specific. Would you please not say I want to get small enough to wear a particular dress again? Say, I will release 20 pounds by April 1st and start in January.

For *Measurable*, how will you measure your progress? Will you weigh yourself monthly; will you take body measurements at the beginning, middle, and end? How will you know that you are moving towards success?

For *Achievable*, your goal must be possible and not so hard that you cannot reach it. It also must be worthy and significant. For example, if you set specific goals on how you plan to release 20 pounds, you should follow your plan and reach your goal. Do not create a goal to release 20 pounds in one week, as that is not achievable. How do you plan to release the 20 pounds? Will you exercise five days a week? Will you intermittent fast; what exactly is your plan?

Your goal must be *Rewarding*. What will you obtain or receive when you release the 20 pounds? Will you be able to fit clothes you could not before? Will you have normal blood pressure? Make sure your goals reward you.

Lastly, your goal must be *Timely*. A specific timeframe with a start and finish date. For example, you can release seven pounds per month. That said, your overall goal is to remove 20 pounds.

Reaching goals boost your confidence as they show you just how great you are. It is one thing to say you are great, but you start to believe it when you prove it to yourself.

Imagine creating a goal such as going back to school and obtaining your high school diploma or doctoral degree. We know how complex both tasks are; so much work, determination, discipline, and focus are necessary. You will more than likely create fears in your head, such as what if I don't pass? What if I go through all this work and cannot write a dissertation? You will have many what-ifs? If you give any of those *what if's* energy, you will quit and feel like a loser. But what if you ignore those fears, persevere, and obtain your degree? How would you feel? Would you believe in yourself? Would your confidence fly through the roof? I think you will. Do you see why setting SMART goals are crucial in boosting your confidence and creating a better version of yourself?

Before you document your SMART goals, I will share one of my past dreams.

SMART Goals

Specific: I will obtain my L.L.C. by March 2019.

Measurable: I will pay the attorney fees by January 2019 and have all documents ready.

Achievable: I will complete all necessary forms and answer all questions needed for my filing attorney.

Rewarding: Expanded business, contracts, joint ventures with other companies, potential grants for my business.

Timely: January 3rd, 2019 – March 1st, 2019 *Goal obtained.*

Think about it as this is no hurry. Focus and gain clarity on a tangible goal. Do not take this lightly. Remember, the purpose of this book is to build a better you, and for that to happen, you must take this work seriously. Writing SMART goals is an excellent way to increase your confidence, thereby creating a better you. Just remember, start with something small but meaningful. Once you reach your first goal, make another one. Always be sure to write your goals down and read them daily. You want to stay focused on your goals as we all tend to create distractions or, as most say, become distracted by life. At any rate, reaching goals will make anyone feel well as once you obtain your desire, you feel good and believe you can achieve whatever you believe. Hence, the book's goal is to empower you to think that you can have, do, and be whatever you choose. Raise the bar. Shoot for that goal you wanted to reach, but fear stopped you.

Chapter Five: Fears and Desires

You cannot release or overcome what you refuse to face. On the other side of fear is opportunities, but how would you know if you never move forward. Check this out.

I watched a movie entitled 'Mine,' and it was about a young boy (Mike) who watched his father physically abuse his mother. His father also physically harmed him. In case you have not watched the movie, prepare for a spoiler alert.

As an adult, Mike confessed his love on bended knee to his girlfriend, and she assumed he was about to pop the question and responded yes. Mike replied, yes, what? You can see the pain in her face and confusion on his. That moment turned into an explosive argument as Mike almost became his father. Mike was afraid of becoming his father. In a reactive rage, Mike decided to leave and join the marine. After an incomplete mission,

Mike stepped on a mine and was given 52 hours by his team before rescuing him. That was his last step before death in Mike's mind, so he refused to take any more steps ahead. During those 52 hours, Mike became dehydrated, wolves attacked him, someone shot at him, a sandstorm beat him, and an African man teased and guided him to the help of his dead daughter's spirit.

    Mike was afraid he would die or lose his legs as his partner did. The African man advised Mike several times to take the next step forward and remove the fear. Instead, Mike chose to stay on his bended knee with his foot planted on top of the mine. He thought of his childhood pain and the end of his relationship. Mike realized that joining the marine was an escape from his father. He also learned that he was stuck on the mine because he never got over the pain from watching his father beat his mother and him. His body moved forward, but he never released his pain.

To make this hour and a half long movie short, Mike's fear of dying and being without legs imprisoned him for over 52 hours in a desert. He never took the next step forward, even at the request of the African man. It was Mike's dehydration and surrender that led to his fall. Mike surrendered to his fears and pain and was free to go home. He proposed to his girlfriend at the airport. He was on bended knee for over 52 hours and immediately went back to the bended knee when he saw his girlfriend. Mike faced his deepest fear in the face of pain. Mike feared becoming his father, which led him to the marine, and it was the marine experience that freed him from becoming the man he despised.

On the other side of fear is an opportunity, but you will never know if you do not take the chance. Before I ask you to share your worries, let me break down fear or false evidence appearing real. In the movie, Mike had other concerns besides becoming his father. Mike's other fear was that of being blown up if he took his foot off the mine. Mike's friend was blown up in his face right before Mike took his final step, and that was actual evidence. So, Mike had legitimate evidence to support his fear. However, Mike's friend did not die; he lost both of his legs, and, shot himself to death after that since the pain was excruciating.

Mike feared losing his legs and imagined what life would be like without his legs. The only way Mike would find that out was to take the next step. In essence, his evidence appeared genuine. Again, the only way to find out was if Mike moved forward.

Mike never entertained the thought that maybe he had not stepped on a mine, and due to his fear, he refused to find out. The only evidence Mike had was the noise he heard after stepping on it and watching his best friend get blown up. He was not 100 percent sure that he stood on a mine as it just appeared to him that he did. His African friend knew differently. So, Mike's false evidence appearing real was the clicking noise and watching his friend get blown up.

After being so dehydrated, Mike fell and realized he was standing on a can and not a mine. His false evidence appeared real and confined him to a space that almost cost him his life as numerous wolves attacked him and someone shot at him several times. Fear is debilitating and leads to humans' death, mentally, emotionally, physically, and spiritually. Be sure to watch 'Mine' on the Google Play streaming app, or it may be on Netflix.

There are two more reasons we need to face and release fears. When we focus on fears, we create more frightening experiences. What you focus on and believe, you attract. What's more, fear is rooted in ego or self-sabotage.

When we focus on the fears such as losing a leg, failing a test, not having the money you need to pay a bill, or being robbed by someone, we attract more fear. I know you probably wonder what that means; well, let me spell it out for you. If you fear someone robbing you while out at night, you will attract someone who needs money and fears not having it or enough. The person who may rob you lives in fear and may need money to buy his kids pampers or feed his drug habit. Either way, his fear exists. Fear is an emotion or energy in motion at the metaphysical level so that the same fear you project into the world will attract other humans living in fear. So that person needs your money to pay a bill or buy pampers, and he robs you as he fears not being able to do so. That is an attraction at the metaphysical level. I hope you now understand or have clarity on why it is essential to acknowledge and release fears. I will share one more example.

If I am concerned about failing a test, I might skip school to avoid the exam. However, not taking the test is a guaranteed failure. That is self-sabotage. Your fears of failing led you to miss school resulting in a guaranteed failure and not knowing if you would have passed. So, what do you do? You focus on your desires. However, for the sake of this book and this section, I will focus on you releasing your fears.

Before I ask you to share yours, I will share a few of mine, old and new.

- I used to be afraid of being alone (not having a man).
- I used to fear not having enough money to pay bills.
- I feared experiencing another healing crisis.

If you notice, the three fears I listed are all in the past tense. If we trust the process of life and know there is only 'good,' what is there to fear? However, if we believe in duality like good and evil, God and the devil, or negative or positive, we create fears based on duality. I understand that all that I experience is for my highest good, and even in the storm, something exceptional is coming.

What's more, if we understand that we are creators, we will accept our experiences and create something beautiful. Instead of focusing on your fears, shift the focus to your desire. If your ego creates a fear that states you will not have enough money to pay your rent, do not give that thought any energy. Create a new idea, such as my income exceeds my expenses. Think and feel it until the fear disappears.

If your mind creates a fear that states you will 'catch' cancer, make a new thought such as 'optimal health.' It is just that simple. But we have been programmed to live in fear. The battle is within your head, not with God, nor the devil. You are either your best self or your own worst nightmare. Your thoughts initiate that thing you focus on or desire. Your emotions amplify that thing, and your actions create that thing. Be careful of what you make.

Be accountable for your creations and stop blaming anyone or thing. If you, did it, you can undo it.

Examples:

Fear	Desire
I used to be afraid of being alone or not having a man	I am always loved and supported
I used to fear not having enough money to pay bills	My income exceeds my expenses.
I feared another healing crisis	I have optimal health.

Chapter Six: Self-Date

Are you one of those people who always must take someone with you when you go out? When was the last time you went on a date alone? When was the last time you ate alone at a restaurant? When was the last time you went to the movies or out of town by yourself? I know you might think, why would anyone want to go out of town and on dates alone? Well, that is why it is called self-date. Self-dating is an opportunity to be with self and get to know self. If you cannot be alone with yourself, do not expect anyone to be alone with you?

Imagine sitting in a restaurant with a nice outfit on as you wait for your food to arrive? Imagine eating your food as you sit with yourself, not on social media, just with you. You may feel uncomfortable initially, but whenever you feel uncomfortable, that is a time of growth. When I felt uneasy about releasing my first book, I had no idea what was going to happen. Once I did my first book signing, I was no longer uncomfortable. It is like graduating from the eighth grade and feeling awkward about high school. You graduated, experienced growth, and now all you must do is experience your first day of high school, and suddenly you are comfortable. Get comfortable with being uncomfortable as it represents expansion.

Self-dating gives you a feeling of certainty and feeling good about being you. Not many people are even interested in sitting by themselves at a restaurant, let alone flying on an airplane by themselves. What's more, what better way to build a better you than by spending time alone? If I can go on vacations by myself, I must believe in my ability to schedule the flight and hotel room; catch the flight, get to my hotel, and do whatever I choose in that state. I must believe that I am capable if I travel alone. I mean, there is quite a bit that goes along with traveling besides the fact of walking through a large airport alone looking for your gate.

Even if it is something as simple as going to the theatre or bowling, imagine the people who will stare at you because you are alone. Their staring is a level of admiration as most people cannot spend time alone as they have no idea how to enjoy themselves. Self-dating is impressive and a sure way to build a better you. When you take yourself on a date, take selfies or ask someone to take pictures of you. The pictures are memories of where you were and how far you have come. Pictures are also a journey to a new you.

The more you spend time alone, the more you appreciate yourself and quality time alone. Doing anything alone takes a significant amount of belief in self. I cannot imagine you not believing in yourself after booking your travel and traveling to and from another state alone. A concert is known to have thousands of people and causes anxiety for people who prefers smaller crowds. You will have to move through all those people to find your seat, buy food, drinks if you desire, use the bathroom as I am sure there will be a line. That is enough to scare anyone into not going to a concert alone. However, if you want to elevate your person, self-dating is an excellent way. Try going to an amusement park alone, and if you make it out alive, you will brag on yourself for years. Try the ultimate fear; jumping out of a perfectly working airplane or skydiving, I did. Try packing up and moving to another state. I did and was traumatized for the first six months. But now, I am over it and enjoying my life in Arizona, for now.

  Lastly, please do not confuse alone with loneliness. Alone is simply being with you, and loneliness comes with sad feelings of being apart from people. Eventually, you will enjoy being and spending time with yourself. As you raise your vibrations, you will see that many humans are filled with negative energy and projecting it into the Universe. And for that reason, you will appreciate being by yourself.

Listed below are some of the activities I have done alone. You are welcome to add more, but these are the ones I thought of or done alone. Don't forget to document the date. You are welcome to replace any of the activities with your choices.

Self-Dating Activities
- Movie
- Dinner
- Bowling
- Skating
- Amusement Park
- Travel
- Shopping
- Concert
- Play

- Ice skating
- Dancing
- Spa
- Hiking
- Read a book in the park
- Skydiving
- Moving to another state

   Please do yourself a favor and try some of the activities from the list. I promise you will thank me later and do not forget to take pictures and applaud yourself.

Chapter Seven: Self-Comparison

Comparing self to others is a definite blow to your confidence as well as your esteem. Your self-esteem and confidence are suffering because you compare yourself to those in the limelight behind closed doors. Would you please stop it?

You must ask yourself why you believe you need to look at someone else as a standard for you. Mainstream and Hollywood created *celebrities* or people that are well known for their work and perceive them as the standard. Standards designed via television or even your upbringing may be beauty, the perfect size, 'good hair,' what success looks like, the perfect eyebrows, round booty, sexy cars, big houses with the white picket fence, and white-collar jobs. Society conditioned us to believe that if we do not measure up to what the mainstream says is the standard, then we are worthless.

Millions of people worldwide have low confidence and self-worth because they are comparing themselves to society's standards.

Societal norming or brainwashing has you thinking your standard is outside of you, and I know that is not true. The only person you should compare yourself to is the person you were yesterday. Who were you at seven, eight, nine, or ten? Who were you as a teenager? Are you the same person, or have you evolved? How can you make another human your standard? You have no idea what their life's journey is, and when God made you, he only made one of you, unless you are a twin. So, therefore your journey is not supposed to be someone else's. You are not supposed to compare yourself to anyone but yourself.

Here are a few reasons you should not compare yourself to anyone. Comparing yourself to someone leads to sadness and misery as you start to wish you were like the person you made your standard. You can also develop envy. Another reason you should not compare yourself to anyone is that no one has a perfect life. Those people you compare yourself to and wish you were, are probably unhappy behind closed doors. Even if they are not, comparing yourself to anyone will destroy your person.

If you spend your time comparing your life, successes, failures, body, hair, or anything about you, to someone else, you will lose out on a lot of time learning about yourself. What's more, you will never get anything productive done. Spend your time wisely and focus on what you desire, not what someone else has. Remember, their life's journey is different from yours. They are where they are supposed to be, and so are you. But the only way to create better for you is to start believing in yourself and stop comparing yourself to what mainstream deems as "all that."

The only reason you should ever make any comparison is for empowerment reasons. If I start a new business, I need to learn from others. So, one of the things you can do is the benchmark. Benchmarking is a tool used to compare business processes to yours for the sake of learning and empowerment. Other than that, I do not see another reason to compare you to another human being. Compare yourself to the past, you and only you.

So let us talk about internal or self-comparison. Internal or self-comparison analyzes the person you were before and then looks at who you are today. For example, ten years ago, I had one published book. Today, I have seven published books. What does that mean? It means I have improved a lot. If you were an angry and bitter person in 2014 and today you are happy and filled with joy, you have made significant progress. If you were obese in 2016 and now lean and defined, would you not say that is excellent progress?

    My point is, why compare yourself to anyone when all you must do is look at the person you were. I guarantee that will make you feel good. If you know you released weight, created more income, ate healthier, and exercised more, you will feel good and cultivate your confidence. Compare self to self as you are the stand for you. Stop seeking approval and acceptance. I understand that maybe as a child, you felt unloved or unwanted; however, you do not have to feel that way today. Maybe someone verbally abused you or your father or mother abandoned you, and you carried those feelings of unworthiness to your adulthood. What your parents, guardians, or otherwise did or said to you had nothing to do with you and everything to do with them. Please understand that children internalize or take everything personally because they have no idea how to let words bounce off you and stick to the sender. But today, it is time for you to create a new narrative for yourself by believing that you are love and abundance at the core. Comparing self to others means you do not value or know thy-self. The way to compare is through "internal competition." Be better than you were yesterday as there should be no one in your mind who you feel is better than you. You are the most important person in your life, and you must start treating yourself as such. Please look at how I compare myself to myself.

Past Me; 38
- I smoked cigarettes
- I slept around irresponsibly
- I was depressed
- I did not value myself

Present Me; 48

- I released cigarettes
- I keep my body to myself
- I am happy
- I understand my worth today

It is no secret that it takes a lot of mental toughness to give up one of the most addictive substances known to humanity. Now, maybe you tried to quit smoking and failed, and that is okay. I tried at least 25 times and finally succeeded on the 26th time. So, self-comparison is a fantastic way to build a better you.

As I reflect on when I was depressed, I rarely took a bath, overate all the time, abused alcohol, cried a lot, and often thought about suicide. Today, I am happy with myself, my life, and all my experiences. The movie "Butterfly Effect" inspired me to accept my past life as if I change anything; I have no idea where I would be today. To change one experience means my current life will not be what it is, and I am grateful for the space I am in today. The person I was is not the person I am today, and upon self-comparison, I would say that I have made tremendous improvement. I have accessed more extraordinary and authentic aspects of myself. I do have more work to do, but at this point, I am happy and honored to be me.

    This section is about evaluating you and actively participating in your growth and development. Being 35 or 45 or even 55 does not mean you have developed emotionally and mentally. You have merely aged biologically, and that is it. However, if you can look at your past self and compare that person to who you are today, you will start to believe in yourself and your efforts. Many of us never even appreciate small growth as we are too busy comparing ourselves to everybody else and what others think we should be or not be. Knowing that you have grown and became better will leave a sweet taste in your mouth as you thirst for more.

In essence, if you compare yourself to yourself, you can determine what other areas need improving. You might ask how. Well, in my previous example, I shared my experience with depression. Depression starts in the gut, leads to the mind, and then expresses itself overtly or covertly. Your thoughts of self and the S.A.D. (Standard American Diet) will make you sad. Another area of my life that needed improvement during that time was my relationship with sex. My relationship with sex was very unhealthy and precarious. I had no inhibitions and had sex with a man or woman on the first night.

I thought sex was a direct connection to love and acceptance, and so I was very sexually active, however, to the point of being unhealthy and irresponsible. Sure, we are welcome to have sex with anyone we chose to;

however, sex comes with a considerable price. We can protect ourselves from sexually transmitted diseases with condoms, but we cannot save ourselves from sexually transmitted demons; or soul-ties. Energy transfers through sex, and since I was very sexually active, I am sure I was stuck with numerous soul-ties. Before getting married, I refrained from sex for seven months or more, and that was my way of learning to create a healthy relationship with sex. I also realized that sex was just sex and not a connection to love. My point, if we self-compare, we can analyze other parts of self and make the necessary transformations. Without looking at self, self-comparison is obsolete. For some, self-reflection is very difficult as most people have been taught to blame and have not accepted those not-so-great aspects of self.

So go ahead and pick a time in your life where you know you needed transformation and examine where you are today. Did you grow? Are you stagnant? Be conscious and aware of your thoughts. If you start to compare yourself to anyone, STOP and remember that you are the standard.

Chapter Eight: Self-Reflection

Greater self-awareness could be the secret to success. It is time to get to know yourself better. Self-reflection is the ability to witness and evaluate our own cognitive, emotional, and behavioral processes. Some therapists and psychologists used reflective awareness and reflective consciousness interchangeably.

Even as you read this book, you probably think about how the book is changing your life or how much time you have left. Can you focus? Are the words clear? Do you feel rushed? Even as I write, I am thinking about receiving the draft copy in my hands, and I am not finished (lol). Self-reflection helps you understand who you are, your values, and why you think, feel, and act the way you do. As we look at self-reflection, a more profound aspect is looking at our thoughts, defined by psychologists as metacognition. Metacognition is the ability to think about our thoughts.

For example, if you think sacrificing yourself is a noble thing to do. Think about where you learned that value or idea. If you think drinking cow milk is healthy for you, think about who taught you that and why humans drink animal excretions. Being able to turn our thoughts on ourselves is a defining feature of being human. Your thoughts are yours, but where did they originate, and how are they affecting you. Thoughts are beliefs and rooted in your core values. But we often overlook the power our thoughts have in shaping our lives, and that is for good and ill. Self-awareness is imperative to happiness, success, and health (physical and mental). When practicing metacognition, one can identify if their thoughts are empowering, harming, or leading us in the right or wrong direction.

  Self-reflecting on our thoughts leads to identifying emotions and behaviors. Your thoughts will initiate a thing or experience, and your feelings will amplify it.

Remember, a belief is a thought repeated. The only reason you believe cow's titty excretion (milk) provides calcium and vitamin D is that commercial actors told you that cow's 'milk' provides calcium and vitamin D. And 'Milk it Does a Body Good." Wrong. Cow milk weakens humans' bones by depleting them of calcium, causing a drop in the ph. Once the pH has dropped, the body pulls calcium from the bones to create balance, and over time causing softening of your bones or osteoporosis. That said, older women do not fall and break their hip; their hops broke, and then they fell. "Milk" also causes skin disorders. Repeat that to yourself repeatedly, and you will believe it. Your thoughts govern your whole life. Remember a time when you left a toxic relationship. Your heart may have wanted you to go back, but your mind's thoughts kept you from going back. What kind of thoughts would prevent you from going back to a negative relationship?

I deserve better. I am valuable. I can do better without them, or I love myself today. Whatever those thoughts were, they guided you and kept you from going backward. Your thoughts protected and kept you safe. If that is the case, then your thoughts can guide you to harm as well.

Everything starts in your head so let me share another example. If you and your significant other argued and shared harmful words, an action or behavior eventually follows the emotion. But, first, in your head, what were you thinking? Were you thinking, *you're not going to talk to me like that, or how can they speak to me like that*, or you were thinking of the next mean thing to say and cut a hole in your partner? Either way, that thought elicited the same angry energy.

Have you ever seen a happy or smiling person stomp a dog? I certainly hope not, as you may have watched a sociopath in action. At any rate, your angry thoughts preceded an emotion, and then maybe the behavior was to slap your partner or to run out of the house. Either way, it started in your head, so you do not get to blame your partner. In accusing, you might say something like this; I slapped them because they disrespected me. I ran out of the house because they made me mad. The truth be told, you lost control besides a few other things.

First and foremost, you allowed someone's opinion of you to penetrate you. Secondly, you became angry as you must have believed what was said to be true about you. Finally, you swung on your partner or ran out the door. Your thoughts and perception of what was said made you angry, not your partner. That said, he who angers you controls you. Who swung, who ran out the door, and why were you running? Whose fist or hand did you use to hit your partner? You used your hand. No one told you to swing other than the initial thought that led to your angry emotion that created the behavior, violence, and withdrawal. Or some core value (beliefs that guide or motivate attitudes or actions) about responding to conflict. You do not get to blame anyone for losing control and lacking the ability to stay calm and communicate or not communicate. You are the only one responsible for you, your thoughts, emotions, and behaviors. Self-reflection and metacognition build a better you by helping you identify sabotaging thoughts and releasing them.

We are creators, and we create the moment we think, feel, and behave. Please stop making discord in your life and blaming others. Thoughts create things. Your mind's eye has no way of determining if what is in your head is real or not, so, *'real,'* it will be. The 'right' brain begins to create what we hold in our heads immediately. Start paying attention to what you are thinking.

When running from explosive situations, we run from ourselves. When you ran out the door or from that relationship, who left and who calmed down? You did. You're fleeing your shadow self or those parts of yourself that are not accepted. Self-reflection allows you to notice the flaws in your personality. Increasing our self-awareness enhances our decision-making, makes us more alert of fake news, and enables us to think more clearly under pressure. In many areas of life, metacognition can be the difference between failure and success.

Ask yourself; What am I thinking, and what am I feeling. Why do I refuse to look at my thoughts? Do my thoughts create emotions? Have I been taught that everything about me is bad or wrong, and did I believe the negative opinions that others said about me? What is it about me that I refuse to look at, and why? What are my core beliefs, and where do they originate? What am I thinking? Am I harming myself with my thought pattern?

Often, we blame others rather than look at ourselves because it is easier to avoid looking at our truth. Imagine not criticizing yourself when you did things that were "wrong" or caused harm to other people. Imagine looking at those parts of you so that you can learn to heal and accept yourself. If you continue to avoid yourself, you will never reach your best self. In those parts of you that are in pain or suffering is your best self. However, it will take you to self-reflect on the person you were and are.

Share some of your negative and positive thoughts for this exercise, and then document the corresponding emotions and potential behavior. For example, if you think all women are liars and all men are honest, what emotions follow those thoughts. Here is an opportunity to look at yourself.

Thought	Emotion	Behavior
Women are liars	Anger, sadness	Insecure, possessive

Thought	Emotion	Behavior
Men are honest	Happiness, joy	Secure, unselfish, permissive

If you think all women or men are cheaters and no good, it is time to analyze why you have those thoughts. Is it the people you have dated that have shown you deceitful or "bad" behaviors, and now in your mind, all men or women are no good? What are you thinking? What man or woman hurt your feelings? Was it your mother or father? Why are you still angry at an ex? Why do you believe you are a victim in your life, and you have the leading role? Ask yourself these questions as the solution will help you see yourself and where your thoughts originate.

If you believe you are worthless, ask yourself why and how? How much of what you think about yourself is what some else said? I am confident that those people who criticized you were loved ones.

What is more, your parents may have criticized you for not doing things the way they wanted you to. Maybe your teachers criticized you or your friends, and now all you do is knock yourself. How can Also, with all the criticism, you decided that you were worthless. You made that decision, not anyone else. You were probably never praised for your good efforts, and with that, the proof is in the pudding. You believe you are worthless. I beg to differ.

You are a beautiful soul experiencing the human experience. The only way to think and feel worthy is to look at your thoughts. Once you look at your choices, you can find the lesson or something you could have done differently and learn from it. The more you avoid yourself, the more you remain stagnant. Self-reflection is being vulnerable enough to look at those unhealthy thoughts and identify where they originate.

Do this.

Sit back and relax for about 30 minutes; no TV, no internet, no phone, no nothing, just you and your thoughts. What are you thinking? Write your thoughts down, and then identify why you believe them. How much of your life have you sabotaged and blamed someone else? For example, when I met my ex-husband, I called, invited out, planned dates, etc. I wore myself out. Now, it is ten years later, and just being cordial to him, I was doing the same thing. However, it took me *one* day to realize that I was repeating the same behaviors that created resentment in me for him. Immediately, I stopped and shared with him, "if you want a friendship with me, you're going to have to call and invite me out; otherwise, you will not hear from me again." Do you understand where I am going with this? I took the time to examine my thoughts, emotions, and behaviors and what I came up with is a part of me is an over-extender, and that is problematic for me. I cannot expect anyone to be me, to me. Self-reflect and correct. He was who he is before meeting me, and I cannot be upset at him for taking what I offered.

    Nevertheless, the solutions are within you and me, and until you look at yourself, you will continue to repeat behaviors and then become angry when humans don't respond the way you want them to. Self-reflect and correct. You know what they say about insanity, doing the same things and expecting a different result.

Lastly, I know someone taught you to believe that Jesus, Allah, Buddha, or Jehovah controls your life and will save you, which is fine if that is your belief. If your thoughts are what I call "stinking thinking," what exactly do you think your emotions are, just as stinky? No one can save you from your thoughts but you. Transform your mind, and you transform your entire life. Do not be conformed to this world but transformed by the renewal of your mind. Even the Bible advises you to renew your mind. Your mind has the power to build or destroy you. What are you willing to do to build a better you? Start with the exercises within this book.

Chapter Nine: Mirror Work

Mirror work is my absolute favorite tool in the world. I love mirror work as you can speak to yourself daily. Mirror work is a process that requires you to look at yourself in the mirror and affirm self-love, greatness, peace, or whatever else you desire. Mirror work is also accepting and loving yourself in the face of those bad experiences. For example, my marriage ended, and it would be easy for me to criticize myself, him and find everything wrong. However, what if I said to the mirror, "it's okay that your marriage ended, but you are still an amazing woman, and something beautiful is coming." After speaking positively to myself, I will feel good and confident about moving forward and new beginnings. However, what if I said, "that was the most horrible relationship, and I hate men." Can you imagine how those words will affect me? More than likely, I will feel the thought "horrible." Mirror work is an opportunity to reflect on self-thoughts and then plant healing ideas that support your confidence and create inner joy.

If you love yourself, you will believe in yourself. Mirror work is not an easy process as most people do not like what the mirror reflects. Many of us are uncomfortable talking to ourselves; saying "*I love you*" isn't something we regularly do. Lastly, your subconscious mind will negate everything you say. For example, if you have always been called stupid, your subconscious mind will reflect that. You say, "I am a brilliant woman;" if you don't believe that, your subconscious mind will say, "I am stupid." Since the last trimester in our mother's womb and up until seven years young, parents, siblings, teachers the windows operating system. Every thought, experience, emotion, behavior, belief, and otherwise is waiting on a trigger.

Mirror work is a daily practice that I learned via the late Louis Hay. When doing the mirror work, you select a few affirmations such as, *I am willing to love and accept myself,* or *I am worthy of love and respect,* and you say it daily while looking in the mirror.

Affirmations are whatever we say or think, and mainly those words that follow *I am*. Whatever follows, *I am*, will follow you. All the dialogues in your head are affirmations. So, if you have a lot of negative self-talk, you affirm those negative things about yourself, which hinders confidence and creates self-hatred. Lack is an illusion as everybody has confidence as it is just a matter of accessing and using it. Do you remember when you learned how to ride a bike or drive a car? You were nervous and felt insecure about success. The only way to master driving a car or riding a bike is to do it. Once you learn, you never forget.

Confidence is within us, and when we put our foot forward, we access, and when we accelerate, we build it.

Your subconscious mind is ready and prepared to accept everything you say about yourself and make it accurate. The subconscious mind is 80 to 90 percent of your stored thoughts, emotions, behaviors, beliefs, and patterns. The more you speak negatively of yourself, the more damage you do. Imagine talking positively to your subconscious mind daily. According to Hay, positive affirmations plant healing thoughts and ideas that support you in developing self-confidence and self-esteem, as well as creating peace of mind and inner joy. The most powerful affirmations are those you say out loud when you are in front of your mirror.

When I was younger, I heard people speak ill of humans who looked at themselves in every mirror they passed. Folks called me arrogant and vain. Like, it was a bad thing to "love on me." I was cursed many times for looking at myself. Even today, in 2021, people criticize others for looking at themselves in the mirror. If you have experienced that, know this, those who criticize you have not accepted themselves as beautiful because someone told them otherwise, and they believed it. Continue to see yourself as beautiful and if you are not in that space, be willing to see yourself as beautiful, loving, and abundant.

    Mirror work has the potential to boost our confidence. Mirror work also reflects what you feel about yourself. Imagine waking at eight o'clock in the morning feeling horrible as you hate your job, recently divorced, and gained 30 pounds; imagine that for one second. When you look in the mirror in the morning, all those unhealthy thoughts and emotions stare back at you, and maybe you begin to cry. Perhaps you shift your thinking and become grateful to be alive or thankful for what your eyes can see. Many of us resist those thoughts and emotions or refuse to acknowledge that they exist and when we do that, they become stronger. You cannot release anything that you refuse to recognize. So, instead of ignoring your reflection, open to what you see and create something that makes you feel good, and that is where the affirmations come into play.

    You can start by saying to the mirror; *I am beautiful and open to loving everything about me* each morning. You don't have to wait until something happens to feel good; create your feel-good. Imagine staring in the mirror and saying, *I am beautiful, unique, and love me.* Can you also imagine the smile and feel-good that follows your affirmations? Maybe not in the beginning, but with practice, you will. When something terrible happens, you immediately feel bad and start criticizing yourself. Instead of feeling bad, go to the mirror and say, everything that occurs in my life is for my highest good and then smile. Smiling is like having sex; it immediately sends a signal to the brain to create joy. Use the mirror to create love and self-acceptance; approve of yourself to the mirror and support yourself via compliments, especially during difficult times. The more you accept yourself and stop seeking acceptance, the better your relationship will be with yourself.

In the beginning, the process was different; however, it was easy for me to say I love you, Kelley, as I was in the space of learning to love myself. You see, not many parents taught their children to love themselves, if any, so do not feel bad for allowing things in your life that did not align with self-love. Do not feel bad for doing something that did not align with self-love. We are right where we are supposed to be now, so whoever or whatever is in your life, they or it is a mirror-image of you. So, do not speak ill of them as you may as well be talking to yourself. It is all good. We all have a story or two or numerous like me.

The significant part about mirror work to me was when my subconscious mind fired back and said, '*you don't love sh***.' I was amazed at how my mind worked against my present moment, and it was not the devil. No, it was not. You were programmed to believe the devil caused you so much pain and hardship when in essence, it is your subconscious mind and the negative programming it received during conception and up until seven years old. Just like a computer downloaded with data or a program, your mind is no different. So, develop a new operating system. If you want to grow, do not blame, be accountable, and be open to learning something new that will remove your limiting beliefs.

When practiced regularly, mirror work can shift your thinking in a matter of 21 days. It takes three weeks to break any habit. Since the pattern is learning to love self and remove self-sabotage, I strongly suggest you trust the words on these pages as your life depends on it, and in fact, it does. That said, when you do mirror work, prepare yourself for your subconscious mind to challenge your positive speaking with a negative rebuttal. Remember, the battle is within. Do not fret; stick to the plan, and eventually, your subconscious mind will believe you, and the shift will occur; a new operating system.

    To this current day, whenever I look into a mirror, I tell myself, I love you, Kelley, you are beautiful, and life loves you. Today, my subconscious mind mirrors what I say. For the next 21 days, I want you to practice loving all of you and releasing things that do not serve you a purpose. Would you please keep a journal of your thoughts, emotions, and body language?

    Journaling is the least expensive way to facilitate and support healing. And as you know, I am all about healing. That said, mirror work is all about reprogramming the subconscious mind to believe you are amazingly abundant, beautiful, and love at the core. So, ask yourself, what are you, who are you, and what do you desire? And then speak it to the mirror for the next 21 days and make it a constant practice.

Again, for example, look in the mirror and say, "I love you (your name) and if you hear a negative thought, respond with say, "I am open to loving myself." Another example is "I am worthy." Do not say I am not worthy as your brain will process "not worthy," and experiences that align with "unworthiness" will present themselves. Keep the affirmation positive and in truth. If you have trouble saying, "I am enough," do not say it. You can replace that with "I am willing to believe I am enough." To sum it up, you can create your affirmations or try the ones below.

Practice every day, five to 15 minutes per day, in a private place where you are uninterrupted. If you become sad or want to cry, release it. Remember, this is about becoming a better you, and crying helps us feel better, thereby becoming better. Below are some of the affirmations I use during mirror work.

- I am safe
- I love myself
- I am open to love myself
- I am lovable
- I accept myself
- I am open to receive
- I am worthy
- I am worthy of love
- I am where I am supposed to be
- The Universe supports me
- I am beautiful
- I am abundant

- I believe in myself
- I am building a better me
- It's okay to feel scared
- I embrace my fears
- I trust the process of life

Again, you are welcome to create what aligns with you. So, get to work.

Chapter Ten: Control, Alt, Delete

Are you familiar with Ctrl, Alt, Delete on your computer? If not, 'Ctrl, Alt, Delete' will reboot your computer's operating system or shut it down and restart it. Additionally, 'Ctrl, Alt, Delete' will also "unstick" a particular application such as Microsoft Word. How does this combination apply to your life? When we use ctrl, alt, and delete, we can reset our mindset by creating alternate thoughts, deleting negativity, or anything person, place, or thing that does not serve as a higher good. That said, let us begin with Ctrl or control.

Control:

Controlling your person means not being reactive. A reactive person responds to a situation or dialogue without thought. The reaction is from a mental and emotional pace that reminds them of a past situation or conversation. For example, I worked with a client who was previously locked in a dark closet regularly as a child. Can you imagine the trauma my client felt as a child? As an adult, my client was married, and he and his wife argued. His wife asked him to leave the house, and when he left, she put the latch on the door. My client kicked the door off the hinges. Upon discussing this situation, my client discovered that the door latch triggered him to his childhood trauma.

    I will use one of my experiences of being reactive. My mother left my father when I was 13. When she left, I felt abandoned, unprotected, and furious. What's more, my father took me to my older sister's house and left. He told me he couldn't take care of me. I cried for days as I wanted to be with my parents or at least one of them. I felt like I lost the most important people in my life. Later in life, during one of my relationships, my boyfriend and I argued, and he threatened to leave. I planted my body in front of the bedroom door and tried to stop him from going. I used all my strength to stop him, and he threw me on the bed and left. He left, but he came back. In my mind, I thought he was going forever. That moment reminded me of when my parents left, and the fear of being abandoned overwhelmed me, and I reacted. I reacted without thought as the only thing my mind focused on was being abandoned and not allowing him time to leave and cool off. Are you following me? Can you recall a moment in your life when you reacted without thought? Think about that for a moment before moving forward. Identify a time when you responded to someone in anger. Ask yourself, is there a time in my past experiences that reminds me of the recent occurrence?

When you react, you come from a subconscious state of mind or space below the human level, such as the reptile state or reptilian brain. As you know, reptiles, such as snakes react quickly based on your actions. For a human, that is not a suitable space as when you react, you create more problems for yourself. Reactions are, again, from triggers. Triggers are persons, places, or things. If you recall, earlier, I mentioned my client kicking his apartment door in as his wife closed the door and connected the latch. If you are reacting without thought, you are not controlling your person. So, what do you want to do? You want to be proactive. Being proactive means creating a situation by causing something to happen rather than responding to it after it has happened. Some examples of being proactive are putting your valuables in a safe space when you know your cousin is a thief. Or don't allow them in your home. Do the action before the occurrence takes place, and you will not have to react. Another example of being proactive is to ask questions. If you are unsure what a person means during a dialogue, don't react; ask questions. In essence, you want to prevent responding to a situation in 2021, with the emotional heat from something that occurred in 1999. Know your triggers.

Alt:

The second task is 'Alt.' Alt is about creating new thoughts. Thoughts become things, so now it is time for you to be intentional with your thoughts. Your thoughts initiate a thing. What is that thing, you ask? That thing is whatever you think or place your focus. For example. If you think "I am a success," well, your right brain will automatically start to create and align your life with what you believe. A belief is a thought repeated. Hence, the reason all 99 news channels repeat the same information, such as that Covid is a deadly virus, but all you need to do is wear a mask and stand six feet away from humans, and you are safe. Really?

Another example is when Hollywood pays a human to say that cow breast excretions supply humans with vitamin D or calcium. Another example is when Hollywood pays humans to read prompts that say that we need animal meat for protein. Are you following me? Have you ever purchased a car, and on your first day out driving, it seemed like everyone was driving the same car as you saw your car everywhere? Well, your make and model has always been present. The issue is you just became present to the vehicle. You might ask, what is my point? My point is when you are present to what you desire, it will appear. If you are present with negative thoughts, negative experiences will align with what you believe. Have you ever experienced something and then said, *I knew that would happen*? Well, it happened because you thought it. At this time, you should realize how important it is to create alternate thoughts. When you believe all men are good, generous, honest, and humble, you will attract those types of men. You are what you think, just as you are what you eat. We have about 60,000 to 70,000 thoughts per day, and most of them are negative. So how do creating alternate perceptions create a better you?

Creating alternate thoughts or positive thoughts initiates that thing you desire. The feeling that follows the idea amplifies that thing, and the behavior makes it. For example, positive feelings and behaviors will follow if you think or believe you are fit and healthy. The emotion that aligns with being fit and healthy is good and confident. The behaviors are doing all things to maintain that healthy body, like eating nutritious food, less snacking, exercising, drinking plenty of water, and so forth. However, suppose you thought you were fat and unhealthy? The feeling is sadness, and the behavior is eating junk food, not exercising, not drinking enough water, and eating poor nutrition. Your emotions and behaviors validate your thoughts.

If you want abundance and success, think about it, believe it, and you will receive it. We are creators, and if you look at your life, it reflects your thoughts. Take, for example, every woman or man you have dated were foul-mouthed, cheaters, liars, and gold-diggers. Your thoughts summons those humans into your life. And if you do not believe me, try focusing on one positive thought for 21 days as you will do during mirror work and watch your feelings and behaviors change. Thoughts are like vibrations sent out to the Universe, and the response is, "your wish is my command." The Universe will align more positive experiences to align with your thoughts. And the Universe never says "no."

So, what do you want in your life? Do not give any energy to that which you do not desire. Why are you focusing on men or women with poor characteristics, being broke or unhealthy? Is that what you want? You are in complete control of your mind, and if you energize positive thoughts, you will create a thought-form. When you energize negative thoughts, counteract the negative thought with a positive one. Please do not ignore the thought; acknowledge that it exists and create an alternate one that makes you feel good. If your mind says, I am fat or ugly, respond with, I am beautiful, and my body is sexy, and say it seven times or until the negative thought disappears. Whatever follows the words "I am" will follow you. I am love at the core of my being, so love follows me. I am health, wealth, and success, experiences that align with the latter follow me. Does this make sense to you? Earlier I mentioned that a belief is a thought repeated.

Let me challenge you. Many people believe that diabetes is hereditary. Why? Because the FDA and the healthcare industry work together to keep humans in healing crises. The healthcare educational system, ran by Rockefeller, taught all healthcare students that dis-ease is hereditary. Mainstream or Hollywood paid an actor to stand in front of a video camera and say diabetes is hereditary. So why do you believe diabetes is genetic? Is it because your mother or father had it, or did your parents pass down the same DIEt to you? Your belief system is based on what someone else thought or believed and shared with you, and now you are teaching your children and friends the same beliefs. Are you following me? Other humans pass their thoughts and DIEts down to us, not dis-ease. And if you want to dive deeper into dis-ease, read my book Detox or Diet. Nevertheless, if you create positive thoughts, you will attract positive experiences and build a better you.

Before I move on to Delete, let us examine the word emotion. Motion means movement or momentum, and the 'e' in energy is emotion. Emotions are powerful energy in motion. And when we feel something, whether a positive or negative emotion, we are telling the Universe, we want more. Your wish is my command. Now, imagine intentionally focusing on positivity and creating alternate thoughts. Do you think practicing Alt will build a better you? I think so.

Delete:

When we think of deleting something from our computer, the computer deletes the file permanently. However, you can attempt to recover the file by restoring your settings before the deletion. In real life, the process is pretty much the same. When we delete or remove someone or thing from our lives, we have an option of removing it permanently or going back to retrieve it.

For example, when a relationship ends, many of us delete that person forever. However, some of us go back and allow the person in our lives again. Additionally, let's say you used to eat cheese and discovered that it was the cause of constipation, skin issues, and hormonal disruption; you might stop eating cheese forever; permanent deletion. However, if you decide to eat cheese once a month, you are retrieving it for consumption.

People, places, things must be deleted or removed to build a better you. We know that negative energy surrounds us, and unless you change the way you think, you will always attract it. Characteristics of a negative person include selfishness, telling lies, gossiping, refusing to admit they are wrong, constantly creating drama, rarely saying anything nice about other humans, life happens to them and not for them, and unforgiving. Does this description sound like you? If so, removing anything must start with you first. When it comes to people, feel free to include family. Deleting family may be complicated because we love them and are deeply connected; however, we can limit our interaction and disengage if they behave negatively. Those relationships with negative people are a mirror image of who you are. I know that may be not easy to accept; however, if you are willing to be honest with yourself, building a better you become easy. No one is in your life by chance but by your thoughts and beliefs. We attract that which we are, believe, and judge. That said, take a survey of those people in your life that have those mentioned characteristics and decide whether you are prepared to delete them or limit your interactions. If you have four negative-minded people in your life, then you are the fifth.

    Do not worry about people judging you for removing them from your life. You do not owe anyone anything, but you owe yourself everything. You deserve positive people in your life and those who hold you accountable for your behaviors and goals. No one becomes better on their own, but you must decide to become better. And with that, you must make the necessary adjustments. Have you ever left your home feeling like a winner, went to work, or just out in the world, and suddenly, you were angry, sad, or confused? More than likely, you met someone negative, and they transferred their energy onto you. Now, imagine a circle of positive friends. Imagine how you would feel with people that spoke and behave positively. It will take deleting all negative humans from your life if you want to build a better you, or at least limit your interactions; otherwise, you will continue to sabotage your life and blame others.

Most of the humans in my life were negative, and I mirrored them. We all came from similar upbringings, and our environments were very chaotic. We are products of our environment, and our negative mindsets and behaviors stem from childhood, as do our relationships with other humans. We gossiped, complained, lied, fought, feared not having enough, or lacked an abundance mindset, and we more than often blamed everyone else for how we thought, felt, and behaved. The unfortunate part about these harmful behaviors is that you and I carried them into adulthood without interventions.

For four decades, I carried heavy, dense, and low vibrational energy. When I decided to clean up my circle, not one person remained. Today, I invite new, positive, loving, kind, and compassionate people into my circle. So, again who are we deleting from our lives or limiting contact? Do the work and take an inventory of your behaviors and the people that surround you.

The humans you delete can be siblings, friends, associates, and even your children. Deleting might sound harsh, but would you allow someone to stay in your life if they constantly beat you or humiliated you in public? Would you allow someone to remain in your life if they told lies about you? Think about this for a moment. The people in your life are mirror-image of you so when you delete them, be prepared to delete the toxic behaviors in you that attracted them. I do not care if these people have been around since childhood, nor do I care if they are family members. Any human who does not serve you a higher purpose, what is their mission in your life? Are they there to teach you about you, are they there to drain your energy, or are they there to build a better you?

  How do you expect to build a better you if everyone in your circle speaks negatively, engage in dishonest behaviors, or never has anything nice to say? How do you create a better you when surrounded by humans who never hold you accountable? Negative-minded humans live negative lifestyles, and if that is what you want or think you deserve, then so it is. So, what do I do if I find myself in the company of negative-minded gossipers? I either sit silently or respond, "Everyone is going through something, so let's not judge or criticize." Sit silently and breathe as your subconscious mind is on autopilot and prepared to spew venom. Tread light when you are in the company of negative people or remove yourself because you can never avoid them unless you become a hermit.

    Today, I do not have many people in my circle, and those who are, are like-minded individuals who aim to raise their vibrations through accountability, self-reflection, and every tool in this book. Those are the types of people you want in your life. Those people can help you become a better person. Anyone else, ask yourself, how can they help you elevate and advance and vice versa? Keep in mind; you want to help others improve if you have that trait within you. If not, focus on you.

    When we look at things, believe it or not, things hold energy. Take an inventory of the items in your house. Do you become angered when looking at specific objects in your space? Are you reminded of hurtful experiences, or do those things trigger you to speak ill? If so, those things hold negative energy, and it is time for you to remove them from your space. Look around your home for broken things as they have broken power and will not serve you a purpose. Stolen items attract humans that will steal. If you have anything from an ex or anyone who hurt you, remove them as the energy will constantly remind you of old pain. Yes, this work is necessary if you plan on creating a new narrative in your life.

 One of my former clients, I will call her Sue, told me she did not understand why she always felt angry in her bedroom during our sessions. Of all the rooms in her home, the place where she was supposed to relax and sleep, she felt the most uncomfortable. I asked her to name all the things in her bedroom, and she stated she still had some of her ex's shoes and clothing. I told her to grab a bag, pack all his items, put them in the bag, and donate them to the Salvation Army. During our following session, I asked her how she felt in her bedroom. She replied, very peaceful and had no idea that things harbor energy. It is the memories attached to the things that create a feeling of discomfort or negative thoughts. Sue said *she could not believe all this time she felt angry and down was because she still had that man's stuff* in her house. Once removed, she immediately felt better. If anything in your house triggers a bad memory or triggers negative thoughts, remove those things. Places or locations are no different. It does not have to be a place that triggers a negative thought, as it can be a place that your soul does not feel comfortable being. Have you ever visited a site where the energy was heavy, and instantly, your person shifted to negativity? If so, do not visit that place again. Go to places that trigger a feel-good. Feeling good means you have good thoughts, and that is your end goal. If you know a particular area will drain your energy; whether it is a club, someone's house, or even an old job, do not visit them. I know you may be thinking, what about a cemetery? Cemeteries are known to create sad thoughts and emotions as your loved ones are no longer here. However, that is different; do not stay anywhere where your thoughts create sadness, and your energy becomes drained. Visit and leave. Not to mention, your loved one is not there physically as bodies decompose, but the energy never dies.

In essence, control your reactions, create alternate thoughts for the negative ones and delete or limit interactions with negative people, places, and things. Lastly, be prepared to delete those toxic thoughts, emotions, and behaviors that attracted the unhealthy energy initially.

Once you have accomplished this approach, you automatically feel good because positive energy surrounds you. I am not aware of anyone who does not feel good when surrounded by healthy energy. Feeling good attracts more when we consciously decide to repeat those behaviors that make us feel good. Lastly, when we remove those negative things from our lives, we create faith and belief that we deserve better, thereby building a better person.

In essence, this assignment requires daily attention to your thoughts, reactions, and attention to those people, places, and things in your life.

Chapter Eleven: Accountability

When most people hear the word accountability, we automatically assume someone blames us or says you are at fault. Well, there is a difference between the two. However, before I share the difference, let me share that I do not believe in fault, blame, shame, embarrassment, right or wrong. Those terms are associated with judgment, and none of us live a perfect life. That said, accountability is merely admitting that you played a part in your experience, outcome, or otherwise. For example, in relationships, people show us who they are, and most of the time, we do not believe them. What I mean is if a woman lies to her man at the beginning of their relationship and he discovers it, what does he expect to occur throughout the relationship? He cannot become angered if she continues to lie as she showed him who she was. Who is accountable if a man pushes his woman a week after dating her and punches her a month later? The man is responsible for pushing her using his hands. The woman is responsible for staying after he used force with her. We must be accountable for our parts in everything we experience.

No one is responsible for what or how anyone thinks, feels, and behaves. We trigger people to a subconscious place in our minds, and then the reaction appears. But that does not make someone else responsible for how you react. Many of our parents did not teach us to be accountable. Instead, we blamed everyone and things.

Accountability is being responsible for your part in the experience or outcome. We like to be accountable when positive things happen, but we blame and point the finger when negative things happen. When we feed our bodies dead energy like animal meat and by-products like cheese (rotten calf excretions), we eventually experience a healing crisis (sick). We then say our condition is hereditary and therefore blaming our parents for our dis-eased body. I know the healthcare system taught you this; however, there is no truth in it. As mentioned in my book, Detox or DIEt, I did not 'catch' hypothyroidism, early-stage heart disease, high cholesterol, or alopecia. Eating dead animals, processed foods, GMO's, toxic products, feeding the candida yeast with sugars and imbalanced hormones created an acidic environment, where our natural bacteria will flourish and hijack our bodies.

So, how was I accountable? I opened my mouth and ate the food. It does not matter what I knew or did not know. I must be responsible for being ignorant and arm myself with the truth to become a better me.

We also must be accountable for our thoughts, emotions, and behaviors. I thought eating dead cows provided me with protein as I thought cow excretions (milk) provided me with calcium and vitamin D. And so, you know, vitamin D comes from the Sun. Mainstream media taught us those lies for making money and us sick.

How often have you heard someone say, she made me mad, or she made me feel this way, or you are the reason I think this way? Abusive or controlling people use that tactic all the time to shift responsibility. *I punched her in the face because she would not shut up. I called him a bit** because he called me a who**.* How difficult is it to say *I punched them in the mouth because I was angry and lost control or wanted the person to shut up*? How difficult is it to say *I was losing the argument?* Take accountability. You have the leading role in your life, and you are responsible for everything that occurs in it. No, you were not responsible for that rape, sexual abuse, or other sexual or violent crime. However, you are responsible for how you respond to life and people after that.

Mainstream society programmed us with too much misinformation. Society trained us to be victims. We hear our parents say, *you gonna make me beat your butt, or you will make me mad*, and we use these words when we find ourselves in quarrels. We repeat what we heard as children. No one makes you angry. You lose control of your emotions and project them. Our feelings are ours, and we are responsible for how we use them. Finally, if I lived my life blaming everybody for everything that occurred in my life, when do I grow? How do I evolve mentally, emotionally, and spiritually? To become better, we must take responsibility for ourselves.

Being accountable makes room for growth. If I continue to date abusive men, I need to look at myself. What is it about me that I do feel is not deserving or worthy of a loving man? Why do I dislike myself? Who taught me that it was okay to allow a man or woman to beat, disrespect, or humiliate me? What do I believe about men? Did I see physical violence in my home as a child? What types of patterns and experiences did I see as a child? To be accountable, you must look at what you could have done differently. What can you do differently if the situation repeats? Until you get the lesson, your experiences will replicate themselves and follow you.

For example, if someone jumped in front of you in the grocery store line and you pushed them, and they beat you so bad you needed medical attention, are you accountable? Your responsibility lies in you shoving them. That push led to a fight, and you needed medical attention. You would like to say that if they had not jumped in front of me, then I would not have pushed them. If that is true, then you are accountable for the result, a hospital visit. What if you had never shoved the person? What if you just walked to another line? What if? Would you be in the hospital? No, you would probably be at home cooking the food you purchased. But instead, you felt like the person did something to you, so you retaliated. Well, where did it lead you? Your negative thoughts led to your adverse reaction. Your ideas could have been, *oh no s/he didn't, or no this trick did not just jump in front of me, or no you ain't going to gangster me, or I'm not going to let anyone bully me,* and again, you reacted to your thoughts. You responded, and that makes you accountable. So, in essence, you co-created that hospital visit.

What if another teenager beat up yours, and you decided to take it upon yourself and discipline someone else's child? During the parent-teacher conference, the other child's parent gave you a black eye, broke your arm, and now you must miss four weeks from work, which leads to being behind in your bills. Where do you hold yourself accountable? It does not matter that you and your child got beat up. Falling behind in your bills was due to your thoughts and behaviors. You were probably thinking; I *cannot wait to see this kid; I'm going to beat their ass.* Or maybe you thought the kid is a bully, and you wanted to be the judge and juror. Whatever your thoughts were, they led you to that broken arm, four weeks off work, and behind in your bills. Again, what could you have done differently? There is always another approach.

    Imagine having done the complete opposite like talked as civilized adults. You would be at work making your money. The teenagers could have talked things out and moved forward, and you could have discovered the truth of what happened. You would have felt good about the situation, and the youth would have learned a valuable lesson about fighting in school.

Every decision is a creation, whether good or bad; remember it started in your head. When you choose to ignore thoughts that lead to trouble, you boost your confidence as you do not create discord or pain in your life. I think a peaceful life would empower anyone to feel good. In essence, accountability increases your confidence as you grow and not repeat the same lessons. Experiences repeat until you get the lesson. The blame game takes you away as you focus on what the other person did and never see what you could have done differently. If you can look at yourself, you can take a different approach. Would a positive approach make you feel better about yourself?

Have you ever heard a man say, she put me out of the house? I have, and in fact, I have told people to leave my house. No one gets put out. You put yourself by violating boundaries, being abusive, disrespectful, and projecting some other foul behavior. Again, what could you have done differently?

For this exercise, think of three experiences when you blamed someone for something that occurred in your life. After that, you will share your accountability. Remember, you have the leading role. There is no growth and development in talking about what the other person did. However, there is stagnation. The more you discuss what others did to you, the fewer chances you have of building a better you.

I will share one more example of my accountability as it relates to relationships. When I met one of my ex-boyfriends, he reeked of liquor and was not drunk. That is a red flag. What's more, he was very jealous when I talked to other men, envious and he ran the streets every weekend with his boys. He never invited me out on dates; instead, we sat around and drank with his boys. If these instances occurred within the first six months, I should have run. But I did not. So, I was accountable for staying if anything negative or painful happened in that relationship as it was a dead end. I stayed due to not understanding my value and worth. If this rings a bell, you must be accountable or meet the same experience; only he will look differently. Now it is your turn. Think of three occasions when you blamed someone for something that occurred in your life. After that, you will share your accountability. This process might be painful initially, but I guarantee you will build a better you with practice.

Chapter Twelve:
Focus on Solutions, not Problems

No one is problem-free; however, your perception of the issue determines if it is a problem or if your perception is the problem. The Oxford dictionary defined perception as a way of understanding or interpreting something or a mental impression. People also create perception based on sight, touch, taste, smell, and sound. In other words, perception is merely a lens or mindset from which we view people, events, and things. For example, one person may say that baked sweet potato pie smells like their mother's baked bread. That said, how we perceive anything affects our communication. The person smelling the sweet potato pie may say something like, "you're baking the same bread my mother baked when I was young, and she didn't share any with me."

Another example is if you see your wife talking to another man and perceive it as flirting, you might become angered and yell at your girlfriend. However, she may just be educating him or having a typical dialogue. If you see your child running out of the store with a bag in her hand, you might perceive it as stealing. The conversation may include assumptions, accusations, and discipline. In essence, we believe what we perceive to be accurate, and we create our realities based on those perceptions. And although our perceptions feel very real, that doesn't mean they are necessarily factual.

Moving forward, the first thing to make a note of is the word problem. The word problem creates the perception of trouble. That said, let us use the word challenge. Most people perceive a challenge as something to defeat, beat or overcome.

Please note: Words put a spell on us, hence the word spelling.

In life, we all face experiences that will stop us in our tracks as we create fears. However, the only answer for dealing with any issue or challenge is to find a solution. When we focus on problems, we create more experiences that will challenge us. Please understand that challenges, issues, or problems are food for our growth; however, if you do not have that mentality, all life experiences will weigh heavy on you. Ninety-five percent of humans focus on problems as most want to prove a point, be right, have no idea how to solve problems, or are addicted to chaos. Some of us avoid our challenges and completely dismiss that any exists, leading to self-sabotage.

Which one are you? Or are you like me; have a desire to find a solution, learn from it, and move on. Don't get me wrong, depending on the issue and my energy that day, I might spend too much time on the problem, like 30 minutes, and then I check myself and create a solution or lean away from the issue if it does not affect me. For example, my son made beef tacos, and I taught him to rinse the meat off by draining the grease and running it under hot water. He decided not to rinse the melted fat off, and immediately I tried to control the situation. I told him you're not supposed to add the season until you rinse the grease off, and the same way grease will plug a sink, it will clog your arteries. My son said *I decided not to rinse the oil off*, but he was distracted by his phone. Nevertheless, my reaction originated from my old healing crisis and understanding what could happen to his body and how suddenly, I would be responsible for helping him heal or taking him to the doctor. Instead of focusing on the issue, I kindly explained that he could find a way to the emergency room if he becomes ill.

Another example is one week after my graduate school term began, I discovered my son had been stabbed in his lung and kidney, and the surgeons paralyzed him to save his life. There was a tube coming from every hole. I did not panic as I did not foresee death for my son. However, I did a lot of deep breathing as I watched him lying in the ICU bed. Withdrawing from school was not an option; however, I needed to be at the hospital with my son. I decided to pack up my laptop, clothing, and everything I needed and stay at the hospital. Of the six days, I spent four nights and visited the other two. Watching my son lie in a hospital bed was very challenging, but the biggest challenge was not allowing fear to fester in my mind. Had I allowed fear to infiltrate my mind, I would not have focused on school, or received two A's. What's more, I knew my son was scared, so I had to remain in positive spirits to uplift him.

My perception of his experience allowed me to move forward and focus on my life while supporting him. From the beginning, I knew it was a life lesson for my son and me as well. I knew that he would be fine. I did not know how long the recovery would take, but my son recovered fully in about a month. The most important thing I learned during my son's challenging experience was to let my son be as he has his journey. I was so used to trying to help, dictate or control his every move due to fear. As we all know, young Black boys and men are targeted and criminalized for being "Black." Today, I allow my son to be who he is, and if he wants to sag, smoke marijuana, withdraw from school, or whatever else, so be it. Who am I to judge his experience? Hell, I slept with over 100 men, dropped out of college, and went back, smoked a lot of marijuana, and abused alcohol. And look at me today. Do you get my point? Challenges are stepping stones to reach new heights in our lives; however, we will never get the lesson if we choose to ignore them or add fuel to the fire. Focus on solutions and build a better you.

Another example: I had not fully prepared for the move to Arizona. I was so excited to leave Chicago, and the relocation was not inexpensive. Pat and I spent about $4000 moving to Arizona, and after three months, we found ourselves still sleeping on an air mattress, no food, no furniture, barely any toiletries, and no money to pay the phone or light bill and filled with fear. My clientele decreased, and Pat took a pay cut. Shemar was due to come home and had no bed to lie in, and my biggest concern was him having a bed. I had maxed out my credit cards, buying imperative items when we moved in. Besides my cousin, niece, one couple, and a new female associate, we didn't know many people.

I decided to go live on FB and discuss the stabbing of my son, or at least the most I was able to share, and our current situation. After going live and sharing our story with friends and fans, we received about $3000 in financial donations and a house full of furniture. I am still grateful to everyone who supported us.

Sometimes our challenges call for others to step in and assist. Others, we can solve on our own. The most important thing to do is to find a solution. Patrick and I could have blamed each other for our challenges or found fault in everything. I decided to take the wheel and, do otherwise, seek help. And it worked, the end.

What lesson did I learn from that challenge? Ask, and you shall receive as the Universe always provides, and being vulnerable is powerful. How do solving problems boost your confidence? When we solve problems, we add skills to our person. Would you not feel good after solving a problem or defeating a challenge? I think you would. Besides, focusing on the problem or challenge makes you feel bad. When was the last time you had an issue and felt good? Problem-solving creates peace, and peace provokes feeling good, resulting in a better you.

As we live on this earth, challenges will present themselves, and some will be Karma, and if you perceive Karma as a bitch, then what does that say about you. No pun intended. Karma is for personal development and soul healing. Karma is those experiences that present themselves as a mirror to what you projected into the Universe. Chaos addiction will have us focus on the drama and negativity of experiences versus creating a solution. For the next Karmic experience that presents itself to you, stop, breathe, and think about how much toxic energy you want to expel into the Universe and create more Karma.

For example, if you lied to anyone on this planet, expect someone to lie to you. That is Karma; however, the challenge is, that person teaches you not to trust them, and if this person is a child, the issue becomes even more challenging. How does one find a solution to such an experience? Besides not trusting the person anymore, you can kindly remove the person from your space or allow them to be who they are. However, if this person is a child, that solution may not work. We cannot remove children from our space, but we can help them identify why they feel the need to tell lies. Focusing on the person lying will not change anything but assisting them in being honest may help them. Maybe you taught them to lie when the bill collector called, and you told them to say you were not home. Or perhaps when they told the truth, you punished or did not believe them. Either way, the only solution is to accept them for who they are or help them identify why they need to lie to you.

In essence, focusing on solutions decreases stress and builds a better you. So, for this assignment, get a piece of paper and write it down after reacting to your problem. Second, identify what you would like the result or end goal to be. For example, your high school daughter is pregnant. The end goal is for her to finish high school and you not to be the live-in babysitter. The third step is to identify those supportive family and friends, gain access to any community resources. Fourth, please find all the positive you can and help your daughter overcome her pain. You might be afraid of the outcome; however, imagine how your daughter feels. Lastly, leave your emotions out of the experience. Your daughter's emotions are running high and fearful. Do not be an addition to her emotional turmoil. Please focus on the solution, and the only solution is positive support and helping her become the best mom she can be. Anything else is added stress to your body, her body, and the baby. Does that make sense?

Chapter Thirteen: Forgiveness

I cannot stress how important forgiveness is to your overall health. In four of my previous books, I discuss forgiveness and layout steps to the process. With everything I have experienced, if I had not forgiven those that wronged me, there is no way I would have seven published books, a coaching business, online courses, and detox programs and thriving in my overall life. Forgiveness is the key to acceptance and peace. Forgiveness releases you of bitterness, vengeance, and anger. Without forgiveness, you will maintain a victim with a limited mindset seeing everything from a negative perspective. As a result, you will live in fear, with anxiety, possibly depression, and physical dis-ease. Without forgiveness, how do you expect to live your best life? If I had not forgiven myself, I would have continued to feel worthless and allow anything and anyone in my life.

When a child grows up in a painful, toxic, and unhealthy environment, adults' pain becomes comfort or the norm. Forgiveness is key to mental, emotional, and physical health. Forgiveness is key to living a fearless life.

Everybody talks about fight or flight when 95% of humans are living in fear. There is no such thing as living your best life in fear. Your best life does not exist in poor health. Likewise, creating your best life will not happen with limited beliefs. Finally, being happy and healthy is null and void without forgiveness. Have you ever wondered why so many people project anger into the world? Anger is a secondary emotion. So, the question is, what is your source of pain? What are you holding onto or have not forgiven?

I also want to add how unforgiveness negatively impacts your physical body. Unforgiveness carries a lot of low vibrations and leads to physical dis-ease. Those low vibrations include, but are not limited to, anger, fear, vengeance, hatred, resentment, and envy, and that energy leads to anxiety, depression, elevated blood pressure, vascular obstruction, decreased immune response, reduced sleep, chronic pain, and cardiovascular problems. So, in essence, you are destroying your body if you choose not to forgive your wrongdoers.

With that said, I have added what I believe to be the necessary steps to forgiveness to this book.

Cry/ Release

In most cases, humans attempt to ignore the pain. However, your brain will also repress very traumatic events. Instead of dealing with or grieving, they tend to bury it, hoping that it will go away. The problem with that is if the pain is unhealed, you will project that same pain onto someone who had nothing to do with the experience. It is like, bleeding on someone that did not cut you. Now, this leads to more problems because new relationships will be affected. Individuals who have nothing to do with this struggle or pain will feel the wrath from it.

Crying releases pain and allows you to feel to heal. Crying is a sign of life. When a baby is born, the doctor knows the baby is alive because they cried. In the absence of crying, more than likely, the baby was stillborn. Tears are the river to life.

When we do not release our pain, the mind is consumed with negative thoughts, compromising our whole body. What is more, your unhealed pain and trauma dictate your relationships and how you deal with humans if you allow them in your life. You will not be able to love again, not wholeheartedly. So, if you are not sharing love with others, how are you sharing it with yourself. A tarnished heart will always retreat to past pain.

Crying does not mean you are depressed or weak. It means you are strong, vulnerable, and respect your emotions. Do not hold onto the pain. Every tear shed is a sign of strength and freedom to come. So have your five minutes of self-pity and keep going.

Have Compassion

Compassion means to suffer together. When someone hurts you, you desire to help or wish an end to their suffering. You feel motivated to help. Everyone deserves compassion as hurt people, hurt people. I know it is challenging to have empathy for those who wreaked havoc on you. But how many times have you hurt someone? We are all human, and we make mistakes. We have at one point been the villain in someone's life. Whether it was with intent or inadvertently, we harmed someone. How did you feel after you hurt someone, and they held a grudge against you? Deep in your heart, you wanted that person to feel your pain and understand that you needed healing as well. One must realize that this individual needs to heal as well. Therefore, it is now time to investigate your heart and acknowledge that you are not perfect. If you want someone to have compassion for you, be willing to have self-compassion first, as there is no way you can feel empathy for others if not yourself first. Again, everyone has been a villain in someone's life, and that includes you. Humans can only give you want they have. If you squeeze a lemon, you get lemon juice. Engaging or interacting with a negative-minded and scorn human will receive negativity and harmful energy. Therefore, we must all hold compassion. Finally, you must ask yourself how much that person's energy that wronged you is within you? Metaphysically speaking, we attract that which we are, believe, and judge. Lastly, what you put out; you get back.

Acceptance

Acceptance means that what happened; has happened and will not change. When I reflect on my life, incest and sexual abuse will always be there, so accepting it is key to forgiveness. It does not mean that what happened was okay. Accept that you were deeply hurt and left with mental and emotional scars, and some may be physical. Accept the fact that it will be challenging to move forward, but you can and will. Accept the fact that your experiences will always be there. Once you accept your experiences and stop resisting them, you can release them. Resistance brings persistence, and I can speak for you when I say we all desire peace and happiness, but that starts with you.

Be Accountable

Be accountable for your thoughts, behaviors, and emotions. I have discussed accountability in detail in its chapter. When we understand that we all have the leading role in our lives, we stop behaving like victims. Victims think someone did something to them instead of for them. We have always learned from pain, and if we did not, that experience repeats itself. Take an inventory of your exes and write down what they had in common. If you did not identify why you continue to date the same type of person, you did not learn anything about yourself in any of those relationships. You also did not release the belief system that attracted them to you. That starts with you, so you must be accountable for what you believe about men or women and yourself. Your beliefs will present themselves because it is what you believe to be true. I think men and women are amazing and love at the core; however, we are all healing from past traumas. That does not make them bad people. It makes us all human. If you allowed someone to mistreat you, be accountable for allowing such poor treatment and forgive yourself for not feeling like you deserve better. You have the leading role in your life, so stop blaming anyone or thing for your experiences. Everything we experience is for us and not to us. I think I mentioned this earlier. Do you think I would have seven published books without my experiences?

I do not think I would, as I would not have as much knowledge on abuse, health, forgiveness, relationships, and healing. My experiences created the amazing woman behind the words you are reading now. When we allow pain, it is because we are comfortable with it. Well, get uncomfortable, be accountable and learn your worth. Lastly, accountability does not mean you are at fault. It means that you played a role in your experiences. Either your thoughts, emotions, behaviors, or beliefs attracted the experience, so take ownership over yourself and do the work. Stop blaming as it leaves you emotionally and mentally stagnant.

Find Something Positive

Another critical element of forgiveness is to learn from the pain. There is a lesson in everything we experience. For example, what did I learn from my healing crisis? And for those readers who are not aware of my healing crisis, please purchase Detox or DIEt. My healing crisis taught me to raise my vibrations. When humans experience dis-ease, most accept the problem as theirs instead of raising their vibrations and doing something different, like taking control of their health. Instead of accepting alopecia and hypothyroidism as "my" diagnosis, I decided to give my body what is needed to reverse the dis-eased state. What did I learn? I learned that my body was malnourished due to eating blood (meat) and starch (refined carbs). I discovered that my body needed nourishment at the cellular level—nutrition such as minerals like calcium, phosphorus, magnesium, sodium, potassium, chloride, and sulfur. Good fats, proteins, and carbs as well and daily fruits and vegetable is a must. Had I not experienced such a painful occurrence, I would not have worked so hard to create optimal health. Pain is power, and it taught me to treat my body with love and care as it is the only place I must live.

 Although I used a personal, painful experience, learning from your harmful experiences with others is no different. For example, in the past, I have dated numerous emotionally unavailable men, those who lied, cheated, and used physical force. You might wonder what I learned from them well; let me explain. My ex-husband was utterly emotionally unavailable. He had no idea how to process his emotions, so he was angry a lot. He never wanted me to cry, and he would sometimes walk out on me when I cried. The therapeutic world calls that emotionally abusive; well, I call it lacking emotional intelligence. How can anyone be emotionally available to others if they are not in tune with their own emotions? That is the first thing I learned. More importantly, I realized that I am a very patient, understanding, and compassionate woman. I dealt with his energy for nine years, hoping he would hire a therapist and stick with it.

Nevertheless, without the experience with my ex, I would not have a deep understanding of humans who suffer and project their pain. Lastly, I understand what it looks like for a man to be emotionally unavailable, so I released the desire to fix any man. Everyone has a journey to travel, and we have two choices, walk with them, or remove the energy that attracted them so that you do not repeat the experience. I am grateful.

As far as men who use physical force, another ex-boyfriend showed me that my feminine energy was imbalanced. I was too pushy and aggressive, and when that energy meets the male species (not a man), he will use aggression as his masculine energy is toxic and imbalanced. In that situation, I learned to use a more feminine approach to get the response I desire from a man. Nevertheless, I dismissed him mediately after the hit.

Lastly, for men that lie, cheat, and betray, look at yourself and ask, have you ever done the same thing in a past relationship? Do you hold the belief that all men are cheaters and liars? In the past, I cheated on and lied to men. So, who am I to get angry when the energy appears? If I want greatness, then I need to show up great. I hope that makes sense.

When we intentionally seek positive from negative, we find it, heal, mature, and become wiser. Seek, and ye shall find. But if you are constantly seeking negative, you will discover negative. Remember, you have the leading role in your life, so what is present is there for a reason. Trust the process. The final chapter will help you review or rehash experiences that occurred within the day, past week, year, or your entire lifespan.

Chapter Fourteen: Set Boundaries

This process is probably one of the best things I have ever done in my life. Have you ever heard the saying, if you do not stand for something, you fall for anything? Well, that is an excellent way of looking at why boundaries are important. Boundaries are a part of self-care and considered guidelines or limits that one may create to identify fair, trustworthy, and permissible ways other people can behave towards them and how they will respond when someone passes those limits. In a nutshell, personal boundaries are a set of likes and dislikes. When we set boundaries, our needs are met, and we do not experience anger and resentment. Setting boundaries is informing others on how to treat us. Boundaries offer clarity on our expectations, so people know what we want and do not want. Without boundaries, you can expect many arguments, unhappiness, toxic relationships, being run over, and served a plate of hell. I must say, I thought I had boundaries, but if I did, I did not enforce or adhere to them as in the past I accepted such poor treatment. Today, I understand my value and worth, so I set boundaries in my life. I even set boundaries for my son as our children think they are entitled to do whatever and have whatever.

For the sake of clearly understanding boundaries, if you have ever been in a lake or any large body of water, there is always a buoy floating in the water. Swimmers are not allowed to pass the buoy. The buoy is a mark to let swimmers know that dangers may be beyond the buoy. However, in personal boundaries, the buoy is those experiences you prohibit and processes you have set in your life so that others do not harm you.

I believe people will respect our boundaries if we set clear ones. However, an unhealthy individual will do everything they can to resist our boundaries. Some may argue, blame, ignore or even physically harm you.

When you set clear boundaries with other people, if they value you, they will respect them. However, if they do not appreciate you, expect your boundaries to be violated. Expect continuous violation if you do not stand up for yourself and let them know they have crossed a border. Some humans have no idea of what a boundary is as they have not set any for themselves. At any rate, you must decide how you want people to treat you, and setting boundaries teaches people how to treat you. Setting boundaries build a better you as they protect you from physical and emotional harm. They also provide emotional freedom from self-criticism and second-guessing yourself. With limitations, you will not allow harmful energy into your space, and with that, you have no reason to judge or criticize yourself.

Healthy boundaries build a better you by boosting your self-esteem and respect and protecting you from physical and emotional harm. You become assertive and have no problem articulating yes or no, and you have no issues accepting no for an answer. Lastly, you develop the ability to separate your needs, thoughts, feelings, and wants from others and recognize that your boundaries and needs are different from others. By the way, you do not have a right to violate your boundaries as you teach others to do the same. Your boundaries are part of your identity so, do not violate yourself. Your boundaries may hurt others, and that is okay. You have a divine right to protect and preserve yourself. Would you please look at some of my boundaries below?

Relationship Boundaries: (Borders, limitations, or dealbreakers)

- Please do not make me the center of a joke
- Please do not use physical violence with me
- Please do not yell at me
- Please do not call me a bit** or any other demeaning name
- Please do not humiliate me in front of others
- Please do not go through my belongings
- Please do not tell me I cannot change my mind
- Please do not use anything that belongs to me without asking.
- Please do not tell me how to dress or what I should or should not wear.
- Please do not cuss at me.
- Please do not lie or betray me, be honest with me.
- Please do not blame me for your problems.
- Please do not violate my personal space.

Personal Boundaries: (My choice to choose)

- I will cancel a commitment if I am not feeling well.
- It is not my job to save people from their drama.
- I will not accept less than love, respect, care, and trust, even from myself.
- I can spend time alone without explaining to anyone
- I do not need permission to be who I am or think what I think.
- I can say no without explanation.
- I accept no from others.
- I have a right to end draining relationships.
- I have a right to feel what I feel regardless of what someone thinks about my feelings.
- I have a right to speak my mind.
- It is not my responsibility to make sure others are responsible.
- I do not have to answer my phone.
- I have a right to be respected.
- I am not allowed to be in my way.

If you do not have boundaries set, now is the time to create them, so go ahead and build a better you. For this assignment, think about your likes and dislikes. Write them down. Think about how you want to be treated in a relationship and consider those personal boundaries you want for yourself.

Lastly, reflect on your life. Did you ever have boundaries?

Chapter Fifteen: Recapitulation

Recapitulation is reviewing or rehashing experiences or emotions that occurred within the day, past week, year, or your entire lifespan. The purpose behind recapitulation is never to allow experiences or feelings to go unprocessed. When we refuse to feel or work through our emotions, we work our stuff out on other people. We create dis-ease in our body, suppress our authentic self, and destroy relationships. I created 15 questions to ask at the end of each day or week to avoid sabotaging your life. You are welcome to journal your answers that way; you keep up with your emotions and determine if you are evolving or stagnate. See questions on the following page.

1. What is good about this?
2. What is this here to teach me?
3. What are the facts about this situation?
4. What am I choosing to think about this situation?
5. If this was happening for me, why might that be?
6. Who do I choose to be as I experience this situation?
7. How can I use this situation to demonstrate my values and my character?
8. Who do I want to be as I go through this?
9. How do I want to feel, and what can I do to feel this way?
10. What do I have control over here?
11. What don't I have control over here?
12. What strengths do I have that will help me through this?
13. Did I create this situation or experience?
14. Am I overthinking the situation?
15. Am I dramatic or overreacting?

About the Author

Highly dedicated, intuitive, and goal-driven, Kelley R. Porter is a spearheading professional speaker, published author, and life and wellness coach. Her sole mission is to support others in becoming the best versions of themselves that they can be. As a professional with over two decades of collective experience and the founder and owner of Transforming Lives Worldwide since 2008, Kelley has an extensive background within this field and a true ardency for her career. She thoroughly enjoys leveraging her skills to help others unearth their worth and cultivate a healthy mindset to manifest prospering lives.

Growing up on the south side of Chicago in very traumatic circumstances, Kelley discovered early on the vitalness of resilience, commitment, and vulnerability, and those core values are what positioned her to become the inspirational, transparent person she is today. Before establishing Transforming Lives worldwide, Kelley earned an Associate's degree in Medical Laboratory Science, a Bachelor's degree in Health Information Management, and is currently working towards her Master's degree in Social Work, which she plans to complete in the year 2021. Kelley has also written six internationally award-winning self-help books and created an internationally sold skin renewal cream. She has launched detox plans and has been a certified professional speaker since 2017, presenting for countless organizations, including the Robert H. McKinney Law School and the Chicago Police Department.

Kelley has built an impressive resume throughout her career, consisting of 23 years in health care, 15 years as a lab scientist, and has held memberships with the American Society for Clinical Pathologists, the National Society of Leadership and Success, and the Phi Alpha Honor Society. Furthermore, her devotions have not gone unrecognized. She has been featured on several TV and radio stations and iconic magazines such as Rolling Out Magazine, Chicago Tribune, Bean Soup Times, and SisterSpeak237 (Africa). Kelley also obtained numerous awards, with her most recent one being the Woman of Excellence award in 2020.

www.ingramcontent.com/pod-product-compliance
Lightning Source LLC
Chambersburg PA
CBHW070527010526
44110CB00050B/2161